hooked on crochet!
Hats II™

contents

hooked on crochet!
Hats II ™

sans
limites hat

SKILL LEVEL

EASY

FINISHED SIZE
20 inches in circumference

MATERIALS
- Plymouth Encore Tweed medium (worsted) weight yarn (3½ oz/ 200 yds/100g per skein):
    1 skein #0456 spiced pumpkin
- Size H/8/5mm crochet hook or size needed to obtain gauge

GAUGE
15 dc = 4 inches; 8 dc rows = 4 inches

PATTERN NOTE
Join with slip stitch as indicated unless otherwise stated.

SPECIAL STITCH
Puff stitch (puff st): [Yo, insert hook in indicated st or sp, yo and pull through] 4 times, yo and pull through all lps on hook, ch 1.

HAT
Rnd 1: Ch 4, **join** (see Pattern Note) to form a ring, ch 1, 10 sc in ring, join in first sc.

Rnd 2: Ch 2, ***puff st** (see Special Stitch) in next sp between sc, ch 1; rep from * around, join in first puff st. (10 puff sts)

Rnd 3: Ch 1, puff st in first ch-1 sp, ch 1, (puff st, ch 1) twice in next ch-1 sp, *puff st in next ch-1 sp, ch 1, (puff st, ch 1) twice in next ch-1 sp, rep from * around, join in first puff st. (15 puff sts)

Rnd 4: Ch 1, (puff st, ch 1) in each of first 2 ch-1 sps, (puff st, ch 1) twice in next ch-1 sp, *(puff st, ch 1) in each of next 2 ch-1 sps, (puff st, ch 1) twice in next ch-1 sp, rep from * around, join in first puff st. (20 puff sts)

continued on page 20

hooked on crochet!
Hats II

floppy hat

SKILL LEVEL

EASY

FINISHED SIZE
19¼ inches in circumference

MATERIALS
- Annie's Choice medium (worsted) weight yarn (7 oz/328 yds/198g per skein):
  1 skein #AC1000 garnet red
- Sizes I/9/5.5mm and H/8/5mm crochet hooks or sizes needed to obtain gauge
- Yarn needle

GAUGE
I hook: 6½ sc = 2 inches; 8 sc rows = 2 inches

H hook: 8 sc = 2 inches; 9 sc rows = 2 inches

PATTERN NOTE
Join with slip stitch as indicated unless otherwise stated.

HAT
Rnd 1: Using larger hook, ch 4, **join** *(see Pattern Note)* to form a ring, ch 1, 7 sc in ring, join in beg sc.

Rnd 2: Ch 1, 2 sc in each sc around, join in beg sc. *(14 sc)*

Rnd 3: Ch 1, sc in first sc, 2 sc in next sc, *sc in next sc, 2 sc in next sc, rep from * around, join in beg sc. *(21 sc)*

Rnd 4: Ch 1, sc in each of the first 2 sc, 2 sc in next sc, *sc in each of the next 2 sc, 2 sc in next sc, rep from * around, join in beg sc. *(28 sc)*

Rnd 5: Ch 1, sc in each of the first 3 sc, 2 sc in next sc, *sc in each of the next 3 sc, 2 sc in next sc, rep from * around, join in beg sc. *(35 sc)*

continued on page 21

hooked on crochet!™
Hats II™

spring beanie

SKILL LEVEL

EASY

FINISHED SIZE

21 inches in circumference

MATERIALS

- Peaches & Creme medium (worsted) weight yarn (2½ oz/120 yds/70.9g per ball):
  1 ball #01730 bright aqua
- Size G/6/4mm crochet hook or size needed to obtain gauge

GAUGE

15 dc = 4 inches; 8 dc rows = 4 inches

PATTERN NOTE

Join with slip stitch as indicated unless otherwise stated.

HAT

Rnd 1: Ch 4, **join** *(see Pattern Note)* to form a ring, ch 2, [2 dc in ring, ch 2] 4 times, join in first ch-2 sp.

Rnd 2: Ch 6, 4 dc in next ch-2 sp, *ch 4, 4 dc in next ch-2 sp, rep from * around, join in first ch-6 sp.

Rnd 3: Ch 2, (4 dc, ch 2, 4 dc) in first ch-6 sp, ch 4, *(4 dc, ch 2, 4 dc) in next ch-4 sp, ch 4, rep from * around, join in first ch-2 sp.

Rnd 4: Ch 6, 4 dc in next sp, *ch 4, 4 dc in next sp, rep from * around, join in first ch-6 sp.

Rnd 5: Ch 2, 4 dc in first ch-6 sp, ch 4, (4 dc, ch 2, 4 dc) in next ch-4 sp, ch 4, *4 dc in next ch-4 sp, ch 4, (4 dc, ch 2, 4 dc) in next ch-4 sp, ch 4, rep from * around, join in first ch-2 sp.

Rnd 6: Rep rnd 4.

continued on page 23

hooked on crochet!
Hats II

baseball hat

SKILL LEVEL

EASY

FINISHED SIZE

18 inches in circumference

MATERIALS

- Annie's Choice medium (worsted) weight yarn (7 oz/328 yds/198g per skein):
    1 skein #AC1009 goldenrod
- Size H/8/5m crochet hook or size needed to obtain gauge
- 2 buttons
- Sewing needle and thread

GAUGE

7 sc = 2 inches; 8 sc rows = 2 inches

PATTERN NOTE

Join with slip stitch as indicated unless otherwise stated.

HAT

Rnd 1: Ch 4, **join** (*see Pattern Note*) to form a ring, ch 1, 7 sc in ring, join in first sc.

Rnd 2: Ch 1, working in **back lps** (*see Stitch Guide*), 2 sc in each sc around, join in first sc. (*14 sc*)

Rnd 3: Ch 1, working in back lps, sc in first sc, 2 sc in next sc, *sc in next sc, 2 sc in next sc, rep from * around, join in first sc. (*21 sc*)

Rnd 4: Ch 1, working in back lps, sc in each of the first 2 sc, 2 sc in next sc, *sc in each of the next 2 sc, 2 sc in next sc, rep from * around, join in first sc. (*28 sc*)

Rnd 5: Ch 1, working in back lps, sc in each of the first 3 sc, 2 sc in next sc, *sc in each of next 3 sc, 2 sc in next sc, rep from * around, join in first sc. (*35 sc*)

continued on page 24

hooked on crochet!,
Hats II

bow hat

SKILL LEVEL

EASY

FINISHED SIZE
18½ inches in circumference

MATERIALS
- Berroco Vintage medium (worsted) weight yarn (3½ oz/217 yds/100g per skein):
    1 skein #5184 sloe berry
- Size J/10/6mm crochet hook or size needed to obtain gauge
- Yarn needle

GAUGE
7½ sc = 2 inches; 8 sc rows = 2 inches

PATTERN NOTES
Join with slip stitch as indicated unless otherwise stated.

HAT
Rnd 1: Ch 4, **join** (*see Pattern Note*) to form a ring, ch 1, 7 sc in ring, join in first sc.

Rnd 2: Ch 1, working in **back lps** (*see Stitch Guide*), 2 sc in each sc around, join in first sc. (*14 sc*)

Note: Continue working in back lps through rnd 12.

Rnd 3: Ch 1, sc in first sc, 2 sc in next sc, *sc in next sc, 2 sc in next sc, rep from * around, join in first sc. (*21 sc*)

Rnd 4: Ch 1, sc in each of first 2 sc, 2 sc in next sc, *sc in each of next 2 sc, 2 sc in next sc, rep from * around, join in first sc. (*28 sc*)

Rnd 5: Ch 1, sc in each of first 3 sc, 2 sc in next sc, *sc in each of next 3 sc, 2 sc in next sc, rep from * around, join in first sc. (*35 sc*)

continued on page 26

hooked on crochet!
Hats II

banded beanie

SKILL LEVEL

EASY

FINISHED SIZE

18½ inches in circumference

MATERIALS

- Berroco Blackstone Tweed Metallic medium (worsted) weight yarn (1¾ oz/127 yds/50g per skein): 1 skein each #4650 sugar pumpkin (A), #4642 rhubarb (B), #4646 salt water (C) and #4647 nor'easter (D)
- Size J/10/6mm crochet hook or size needed to obtain gauge

GAUGE

6½ dc = 2 inches; 3 dc rows = 2 inches

PATTERN NOTE

Join with slip stitch as indicated unless otherwise stated.

HAT

Rnd 1: With color A, ch 4, **join** (*see Pattern Note*) to form a ring, ch 2, 12 dc in ring, join in first dc.

Rnd 2: Ch 2, **fpdc** (*see Stitch Guide*) around first dc, dc in next sp between dc, *fpdc around next dc, dc in next sp between dc, rep from * 10 more times, join in first fpdc. (*24 sts*)

Rnd 3: Ch 2, 2 fpdc around first fpdc, **bpdc** (*see Stitch Guide*) around next dc, *2 fpdc around next fpdc, bpdc around next dc, rep from * 10 more times, join in first fpdc. (*36 sts*)

Rnd 4: Ch 2, fpdc around each of first 2 fpdc, 2 bpdc around next bpdc, *fpdc around each of next 2 fpdc, 2 bpdc around next bpdc, rep from * 10 more times, join in first fpdc. (*48 sts*)

continued on page 27

hooked on crochet!™
Hats II™

flapper hat

SKILL LEVEL

EASY

FINISHED SIZE
19¼ inches in circumference

MATERIALS
- Annie's Choice medium (worsted) weight yarn (7 oz/328 yds/198g per skein):
  1 skein #AC1036 teal
- Size H/8/5mm crochet hook or size needed to obtain gauge
- Yarn needle

GAUGE
8 sc = 2 inches; 9 sc rows = 2 inches

PATTERN NOTE
Join with slip stitch as indicated unless otherwise stated

HAT
Rnd 1: Ch 4, **join** (*see Pattern Note*) to form a ring, ch 1, 7 sc in ring, join in first sc.

Rnd 2: Ch 1, 2 sc in each sc around, join in first sc. *(14 sc)*

Rnd 3: Ch 1, sc in first sc, 2 sc in next sc, *sc in next sc, 2 sc in next sc, rep from * around, join in first sc. *(21 sc)*

Rnd 4: Ch 1, sc in each of first 2 sc, 2 sc in next sc, *sc in each of next 2 sc, 2 sc in next sc, rep from * around, join in first sc. *(28 sc)*

Rnd 5: Ch 1, sc in each of first 3 sc, 2 sc in next sc, *sc in each of next 3 sc, 2 sc in next sc, rep from * around, join in first sc. *(35 sc)*

Rnd 6: Ch 1, sc in each of first 4 sc, 2 sc in next sc, *sc in each of next 4 sc, 2 sc in next sc, rep from * around, join in first sc. *(42 sc)*

continued on page 28

hooked on crochet!
Hats II

baggier beanie

SKILL LEVEL

EASY

FINISHED SIZE
22 inches in circumference

MATERIALS
- Noro Silk Garden medium (worsted) weight self-striping yarn (1¾ oz/ 109 yds/50g per skein): 2 skeins #341 plum, mustard, tomato, tangerine
- Size J/10/6mm crochet hook or size needed to obtain gauge

GAUGE
7 sc = 2 inches; 9 sc rows = 2 inches

PATTERN NOTE
Join with slip stitch as indicated unless otherwise stated.

HAT
Rnd 1: Ch 4, **join** *(see Pattern Note)* to form a ring, ch 1, 7 sc in ring, join in first sc.

Rnd 2: Ch 1, 2 sc in each sc around, join in first sc. *(14 sc)*

Rnd 3: Ch 1, sc in first sc, 2 sc in next sc, *sc in next sc, 2 sc in next sc, rep from * around, join in first sc. *(21 sc)*

Rnd 4: Ch 1, sc in each of first 2 sc, 2 sc in next sc, *sc in each of next 2 sc, 2 sc in next sc, rep from * around, join in first sc. *(28 sc)*

Rnd 5: Ch 1, sc in each of first 3 sc, 2 sc in next sc, *sc in each of next 3 sc, 2 sc in next sc, rep from * around, join in first sc. *(35 sc)*

Rnd 6: Ch 1, sc in each of first 4 sc, 2 sc in next sc, *sc in each of next 4 sc, 2 sc in next sc, rep from * around, join in first sc. *(42 sc)*

continued on page 29

hooked on crochet!
Hats II

Sans Limites Hat
continued from page 5

Rnd 5: Ch 1, (puff st, ch 1) in each of first 3 ch-1 sps, (puff st, ch 1) twice in next ch-1 sp, *(puff st, ch 1) in each of the next 3 ch-1 sps, (puff st, ch 1) twice in next ch-1 sp, rep from * around, join in first puff st. *(25 puff sts)*

Rnd 6: Ch 1, (puff st, ch 1) in each of first 4 ch-1 sps, (puff st, ch 1) twice in next ch-1 sp, *(puff st, ch 1) in each of next 4 ch-1 sps, (puff st, ch 1) twice in next ch-1 sp, rep from * around, join in first puff st. *(30 puff sts)*

Rnds 7–16: Ch 2, (puff st, ch 1) in each ch-1 sp around.

Rnd 17: Ch 1, sc in each puff st and ch-1 sp around, join in first sc. *(60 sc)*

Rnd 18: Ch 1, sc in each sc around, join in first sc. Do not fasten off.

BILL
Row 1: Ch 1, working in **front lps** *(see Stitch Guide)*, sc in each of first 2 sc, 2 sc in next sc, *sc in each of next 2 sc, 2 sc in next sc, rep from * 3 more times, sc in each of next 2 sc, turn. *(22 sc)*

Row 2: Ch 1, sc in each sc across, hdc in next sc of last rnd of hat, sl st in each of next 2 sc, turn.

Row 3: Ch 1, sk first sl st, sc in next sl st, sc in next hdc, sc in each sc across, hdc in next sc of last rnd of hat, sl st in each of next 2 sc, turn.

Row 4: Ch 1, sk first sl st, sc in next sl st, sc in next hdc, sc in next sc, 2 sc in next sc, *sc in each of next 3 sc, 2 sc in next sc, rep from * 4 more times, sc in each of next 2 sc, hdc in next sc of last rnd of hat, sl st in each of next 2 sc, turn.

Rows 5 & 6: Rep row 3. At end of row 6, fasten off.

Weave in loose ends. ■

Floppy Hat
continued from page 7

Rnd 6: Ch 1, sc in each of the first 4 sc, 2 sc in next sc, *sc in each of the next 4 sc, 2 sc in next sc, rep from * around, join in beg sc. *(42 sc)*

Rnd 7: Ch 1, sc in each of the first 5 sc, 2 sc in next sc, *sc in each of the next 5 sc, 2 sc in next sc, rep from * around, join in beg sc. *(49 sc)*

Rnd 8: Ch 1, sc in each of the first 6 sc, 2 sc in next sc, *sc in each of the next 6 sc, 2 sc in next sc, rep from * around, join in beg sc. *(56 sc)*

Rnd 9: Ch 1, sc in each of the first 7 sc, 2 sc in next sc, *sc in each of the next 7 sc, 2 sc in next sc, rep from * around, join in beg sc. *(63 sc)*

Rnd 10: Ch 1, sc in each sc around, join in beg sc.

Rep rnd 10 until hat measures 7 inches in length.

BRIM
Rnd 1: With smaller hook, ch 1, working in **front lps** *(see Stitch Guide)*, sc in each of the first 8 sc, 2 sc in next sc, *sc in each of the next 8 sc, 2 sc in next sc, rep from * around, join in beg sc. *(70 sc)*

Rnd 2: Ch 1, sc in each of the first 9 sc, 2 sc in next sc, *sc in each of the next 9 sc, 2 sc in next sc, rep from * around, join in beg sc. *(77 sc)*

Rnd 3: Ch 1, sc in each of the first 10 sc, 2 sc in next sc, *sc in each of the next 10 sc, 2 sc in next sc, rep from * around, join in beg sc. *(84 sc)*

Rnd 4: Ch 1, sc in each of the first 11 sc, 2 sc in next sc, *sc in each of the next 11 sc, 2 sc in next sc, rep from * around, join in beg sc. *(91 sc)*

Rnd 5: Ch 1, sc in each of the first 12 sc, 2 sc in next sc, *sc in each of the next 12 sc, 2 sc in next sc, rep from * around, join in beg sc. *(98 sc)*

Rnd 6: Ch 1, sc in each of the first 13 sc, 2 sc in next sc, *sc in each of the next 13 sc, 2 sc in next sc, rep from * around, join in beg sc. *(105 sc)*

Rnd 7: Ch 1, sc in each of the first 14 sc, 2 sc in next sc, *sc in each of the next 14 sc, 2 sc in next sc, rep from * around, join in beg sc. *(112 sc)*

Rnd 8: Ch 1, sc in each of the first 15 sc, 2 sc in next sc, *sc in each of the next 15 sc, 2 sc in next sc, rep from * around, join in beg sc. *(119 sc)*

Rnd 9: Ch 1, sc in each sc around, join in beg sc.

Rnd 10: Ch 1, sc in each of the first 16 sc, 2 sc in next sc, *sc in each of the next 16 sc, 2 sc in next sc, rep from * around, join in beg sc. *(126 sc)*

Rnd 11: Rep rnd 9.

Rnd 12: Ch 1, sc in each of the first 17 sc, 2 sc in next sc, *sc in each of the next 17 sc, 2 sc in next sc, rep from * around, join in beg sc. *(133 sc)*

Rnd 13: Rep rnd 9.

Rnd 14: Ch 1, sc in each of the first 18 sc, 2 sc in next sc, *sc in each of the next 18 sc, 2 sc in next sc, rep from * around, join in beg sc. *(140 sc)*

Rnd 15: Rep rnd 9.

Rnd 16: Ch 1, sc in each of the first 19 sc, 2 sc in next sc, *sc in each of the next 19 sc, 2 sc in next sc, rep from * around, join in beg sc. *(147 sc)*

Rnd 17: Rep rnd 9.

Rnd 18: Ch 1, sc in each of the first 20 sc, 2 sc in next sc, *sc in each of the next 20 sc, 2 sc in next sc, rep from * around, join in beg sc. *(154 sc)*

Rnd 19: Rep rnd 9.

Rnd 20: With larger hook, sl st in each sc around. Fasten off.

Weave in loose ends.

BOW

Row 1: With larger hook, ch 16, sc in 2nd ch from hook and in each rem ch across, turn. *(15 sc)*

Rows 2–10: Ch 1, sc in each sc across, turn. At end of row 10, **do not** fasten off, turn work 90 degrees to begin working Border.

BORDER

Ch 1, sc in each side edge st, turn work 90 degrees, ch 1, sc in each foundation st, turn work 90 degrees, ch 1, sc in each side edge st, turn work 90 degrees, ch 1, sc in each top edge st. Fasten off.

Weave in loose ends.

FINISHING

Cut one 24-inch length of yarn. Wrap around center of rectangle to form bow until 6 inches of yarn rem. Thread tail through yarn needle and continue wrapping, while at the same time sewing bow onto hat.

Weave in loose ends. ■

Spring Beanie
continued from page 9

Rnd 7: Ch 2, 4 dc in first ch-6 sp, ch 4, *4 dc in next ch-4 sp, ch 4, rep from * around, join in first ch-2 sp.

Rnd 8: Rep rnd 4.

Rnds 9–12: [Rep rnds 7 and 8] twice.

Rnd 13: Ch 1, 2 sc in first ch-6 sp, sc in each of next 4 dc, *2 sc in next ch-4 sp, sc in each of next 4 sc, rep from * around, join in first sc. *(72 sc)*

Rnd 14: Ch 1, sc in each sc around, join in first sc.

Rnd 15: Ch 1, sl st in first sc, *sk 2 sc, 5 dc in next sc, sk 2 sc, sl st in next sc, rep from * around. Fasten off.

Weave in loose ends. ∎

Baseball Hat
continued from page 11

Rnd 6: Ch 1, working in back lps, sc in each of first 4 sc, 2 sc in next sc, *sc in each of next 4 sc, 2 sc in next sc, rep from * around, join in first sc. *(42 sc)*

Rnd 7: Ch 1, working in back lps, sc in each of first 5 sc, 2 sc in next sc, *sc in each of next 5 sc, 2 sc in next sc, rep from * around, join in first sc. *(49 sc)*

Rnd 8: Ch 1, working in back lps, sc in each of first 6 sc, 2 sc in next sc, *sc in each of next 6 sc, 2 sc in next sc, rep from * around, join in first sc. *(56 sc)*

Rnd 9: Ch 1, working in back lps, sc in each of first 7 sc, 2 sc in next sc, *sc in each of next 7 sc, 2 sc in next sc, rep from * around, join in first sc. *(63 sc)*

Rnd 10: Ch 1, working in both lps, sc in each sc around, join in first sc.

Note: Continue working in both lps through row 29.

Rnds 11–14: Rep rnd 10.

Rnd 15: Ch 3, sk first sc, *dc in next sc, ch 1, sk next sc, rep from * around, join in 2nd of 3 beg ch. *(31 dc)*

Rnd 16: Ch 1, sc in first ch-1 sp, *sc in next dc, sc in next ch-1 sp; rep from * around, join in first sc. *(63 sc)*

Rnds 17–21: Rep rnd 10.

Rnd 22: Rep rnd 15.

Rnd 23: Rep rnd 16.

Rnds 24–29: Rep rnd 10. **Do not** fasten off.

BILL

Row 1: Ch 1, working in **front lps** (*see Stitch Guide*), sc in first sc, sc in next sc, 2 sc in next sc, *sc in each of next 2 sc, 2 sc in next sc, rep from * 3 more times, sc in each of next 2 sc, turn. (*22 sc*)

Row 2: Ch 1, working in both lps through rem rows, sc in each sc across, hdc in next sc of last rnd of hat, sl st in each of next 2 sc, turn.

Rows 3 & 4: Ch 1, sk 1 sl st, sc in next sl st, sc in next hdc, sc in each sc across, hdc in next sc of last rnd of hat, sl st in each of next 2 sc, turn.

Row 5: Ch 1, sk first sl st, sc in next sl st, sc in next hdc, sc in next sc, 2 sc in next sc, *sc in each of the next 3 sc, 2 sc in next sc, rep from * 5 more times, hdc in next sc of last rnd of hat, sl st in each of next 2 sc, turn.

Row 6: Ch 3, 2 sc in 2nd ch from hook, 2 sc in next ch, sk next sl st, sc in next sl st, sc in next hdc, sc in each of next 35 sc, hdc in next sc of last rnd of hat, turn.

Row 7: Ch 3, 2 sc in 2nd ch from hook, sc in next ch, sc in next hdc, sc in each of next 40 sc, 2 sc in last sc, turn.

Row 8: Ch 3, 2 sc in 2nd ch from hook, sc in next ch, sc in each of next 45 sc, 2 sc in last sc, turn.

Row 9: Ch 3, 2 sc in 2nd ch from hook, sc in next ch, sc in each of next 50 sc, turn.

Row 10: Ch 1, sc in each sc across. Fasten off.

Weave in loose ends.

FINISHING

Fold tabs at the end of bill back onto hat. Using sewing needle and thread, sew tabs to hat; sew a button on each tab, stitching through bottom of hat. ∎

Bow Hat
continued from page 13

Rnd 6: Ch 1, sc in each of first 4 sc, 2 sc in next sc, *sc in each of next 4 sc, 2 sc in next sc, rep from * around, join in first sc. *(42 sc)*

Rnd 7: Ch 1, sc in each of first 5 sc, 2 sc in next sc, *sc in each of next 5 sc, 2 sc in next sc, rep from * around, join in first sc. *(49 sc)*

Rnd 8: Ch 1, sc in each of first 6 sc, 2 sc in next sc, *sc in each of next 6 sc, 2 sc in next sc, rep from * around, join in first sc. *(56 sc)*

Rnd 9: Ch 1, sc in each of first 7 sc, 2 sc in next sc, *sc in each of next 7 sc, 2 sc in next sc, rep from * around, join in first sc. *(63 sc)*

Rnd 10: Ch 1, sc in each sc around, join in first sc.

Rnd 11: Ch 1, sc in each of first 8 sc, 2 sc in next sc, *sc in each of next 8 sc, 2 sc in next sc, rep from * around, join in first sc. *(70 sc)*

Rnd 12: Rep rnd 10.

Rep rnd 12 until hat measures 9½ inches in length for a saggy beanie look. Stop sooner for a more fitted look. At end of last rnd, fasten off.

Weave in loose ends.

BOW
Row 1: Ch 21, sc in 2nd ch from hook and in each rem ch across, turn. *(20 sc)*

Rows 2–14: Ch 1, sc in each sc across, turn. At end of row 14, **do not** fasten off, turn work 90 degrees to begin working border.

BORDER
Ch 1, sc in each side edge st, turn work 90 degrees, ch 1, sc in each foundation st, turn work 90 degrees, ch 1, sc in each side edge st, turn work 90 degrees, ch 1, sc in each top edge st. Fasten off.

Weave in loose ends.

FINISHING
Cut one 24-inch length of yarn.

Wrap this yarn around center of rectangle to form bow until 6 inches of yarn rem. Thread tail through yarn needle and continue wrapping, while at the same time sewing bow onto hat 1–2 inches above bottom edge.

Weave in loose ends. ■

Banded Beanie
continued from page 15

continued from page 15

Rnd 5: Ch 2, fpdc around each of first 2 fpdc, bpdc around each of next 2 bpdc, *fpdc around each of next 2 fpdc, bpdc around each of next 2 bpdc, rep from * 10 more times, join in first fpdc.

Rnd 6: Rep rnd 5.

Change to color B.

Rnd 7: Rep rnd 5.

Rnd 8: Ch 2, 2 fpdc around first fpdc, fpdc around next fpdc, bpdc around each of next 2 bpdc, *2 fpdc around next fpdc, fpdc around next fpdc, bpdc around each of next 2 bpdc, rep from * 10 more times, join in first fpdc. *(60 sts)*

Rnd 9: Ch 2, fpdc around each of first 3 fpdc, bpdc around each of next 2 bpdc, *fpdc around each of next 3 fpdc, bpdc around each of next 2 bpdc, join in first fpdc.

Rnds 10–12: Rep rnd 9.

Change to color C.

Rnds 13–18: Rep rnd 9.

Change to color D.

Rnds 19–23: Rep rnd 9.

Rnds 24–26: Ch 1, sc in each st around, join in first sc. At end of rnd 26, fasten off.

Weave in loose ends. ∎

Flapper Hat
continued from page 17

Rnd 7: Ch 1, sc in each of first 5 sc, 2 sc in next sc, *sc in each of next 5 sc, 2 sc in next sc, rep from * around, join in first sc. (*49 sc*)

Rnd 8: Ch 1, sc in each of first 6 sc, 2 sc in next sc, *sc in each of next 6 sc, 2 sc in next sc, rep from * around, join in first sc. (*56 sc*)

Rnd 9: Ch 1, sc in each of first 7 sc, 2 sc in next sc, *sc in each of next 7 sc, 2 sc in next sc, rep from * around, join in first sc. (*63 sc*)

Rnd 10: Ch 1, sc in each sc around, join in first sc.

Rnd 11: Ch 1, sc in each of first 8 sc, 2 sc in next sc, *sc in each of next 8 sc, 2 sc in next sc, rep from * around, join in first sc. (*70 sc*)

Rnd 12: Rep rnd 10.

Rnd 13: Ch 1, sc in each of first 9 sc, 2 sc in next sc, *sc in each of next 9 sc, 2 sc in next sc, rep from * around, join in first sc. (*77 sc*)

Rnd 14: Rep rnd 10.

Rep rnd 14 until hat measures 5½ inches in length.

Next rnd: Ch 1, working in **back lps** (*see Stitch Guide*), sc in each sc around, join in first sc.

Rep this rnd 4 more times. Do not fasten off.

BILL
Row 1: Ch 1, working in **front lps** (*see Stitch Guide*), sc in each of first 4 sc, 2 sc in next sc, *sc in each of next 4 sc, 2 sc in next sc, rep from * 8 more times, sc in each of next 4 sc, turn. (*64 sc*)

Row 2: Ch 1, working in both lps, sc in each sc across, hdc in next sc of last rnd of hat, sl st in each of next 2 sc, turn.

Row 3: Ch 1, sk first sl st, sc in next sl st, sc in next hdc, sc in each sc across, hdc in next sc of last rnd of hat, sl st in each of next 2 sc, turn.

Row 4: Ch 1, sk first sl st, sc in next sl st, sc in next hdc, sc in each of next 3 sc, 2 sc in next sc, *sc in each of next 5 sc, 2 sc in next sc, rep from * 9 more times, sc in each of last 2 sc, hdc in next sc of last rnd of hat, sl st in each of next 2 sc, turn.

Rows 5–7: Rep row 3. Fasten off.

Weave in loose ends.

BOW
Rnd 1: Ch 30, join to form a ring, being careful not to twist sts, ch 1, sc in each ch around, join in first sc. (*30 sc*)

Rnds 2–6: Ch 1, sc in each sc around, join in first sc. Fasten off.

Weave in loose ends. Flatten to form a rectangle.

FINISHING
Cut one 24-inch length of yarn. Wrap around center of rectangle to form bow until 6 inches of yarn rem. Thread tail through yarn needle and continue wrapping, while at the same time sewing bow onto hat.

Weave in loose ends. ■

Baggier Beanie
continued from page 19

Rnd 7: Ch 1, sc in each of first 5 sc, 2 sc in next sc, *sc in each of next 5 sc, 2 sc in next sc, rep from * around, join in first sc. *(49 sc)*

Rnd 8: Ch 1, sc in each of first 6 sc, 2 sc in next sc, *sc in each of next 6 sc, 2 sc in next sc, rep from * around, join in first sc. *(56 sc)*

Rnd 9: Ch 1, sc in each of first 7 sc, 2 sc in next sc, *sc in each of next 7 sc, 2 sc in next sc, rep from * around, join in first sc. *(63 sc)*

Rnd 10: Ch 1, sc in each sc around, join in first sc.

Rnd 11: Ch 1, sc in each of first 8 sc, 2 sc in next sc, *sc in each of next 8 sc, 2 sc in next sc, rep from * around. *(70 sc)*

Rnd 12: Ch 1, sc in each sc around, join in first sc.

Rnd 13: Ch 1, sc in each of first 9 sc, 2 sc in next sc, *sc in each of next 9 sc, 2 sc in next sc, rep from * around. *(77 sc)*

Rnd 14: Ch 1, sc in each sc around, join in first sc.

Rep rnd 14 until hat measures approximately 7 inches.

Rnd 15: Ch 1, working in back lps, sc in each sc around, join in first sc.

Rep rnd 15 for 2½ inches. Fasten off.

Weave in loose ends. ■

STITCH GUIDE

FOR MORE COMPLETE INFORMATION,
VISIT ANNIESCATALOG.COM/STITCHGUIDE

STITCH ABBREVIATIONS

beg . . . . begin/begins/beginning
bpdc . . . . back post double crochet
bpsc . . . . back post single crochet
bptr . . . . back post treble crochet
CC . . . . contrasting color
ch(s) . . . . chain(s)
ch- . . . . refers to chain or space
previously made (i.e., ch-1 space)
ch sp(s) . . . . chain space(s)
cl(s) . . . . cluster(s)
cm . . . . centimeter(s)
dc . . . . double crochet (singular/plural)
dc dec . . . . double crochet 2 or more
stitches together, as indicated
dec . . . . decrease/decreases/decreasing
dtr . . . . double treble crochet
ext . . . . extended
fpdc . . . . front post double crochet
fpsc . . . . front post single crochet
fptr . . . . front post treble crochet
g . . . . gram(s)
hdc . . . . half double crochet
hdc dec . . . . half double crochet 2 or more
stitches together, as indicated
inc . . . . increase/increases/increasing
lp(s) . . . . loop(s)
MC . . . . main color
mm . . . . millimeter(s)
oz . . . . ounce(s)
pc . . . . popcorn(s)
rem . . . . remain/remains/remaining
rep(s) . . . . repeat(s)
rnd(s) . . . . round(s)
RS . . . . right side
sc . . . . single crochet (singular/plural)
sc dec . . . . single crochet 2 or more
stitches together, as indicated
sk . . . . skip/skipped/skipping
sl st(s) . . . . slip stitch(es)
sp(s) . . . . space(s)/spaced
st(s) . . . . stitch(es)
tog . . . . together
tr . . . . treble crochet
trtr . . . . triple treble
WS . . . . wrong side
yd(s) . . . . yard(s)
yo . . . . yarn over

YARN CONVERSION

OUNCES TO GRAMS		GRAMS TO OUNCES	
1	28.4	25	7/8
2	56.7	40	1 2/3
3	85.0	50	1 3/4
4	113.4	100	3 1/2

UNITED STATES		UNITED KINGDOM
sl st (slip stitch)	=	sc (single crochet)
sc (single crochet)	=	dc (double crochet)
hdc (half double crochet)	=	htr (half treble crochet)
dc (double crochet)	=	tr (treble crochet)
tr (treble crochet)	=	dtr (double treble crochet)
dtr (double treble crochet)	=	ttr (triple treble crochet)
skip	=	miss

Reverse single crochet (reverse sc): Ch 1, sk first st, working from left to right, insert hook in next st from front to back, draw up lp on hook, yo and draw through both lps on hook.

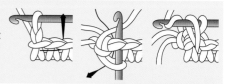

Chain (ch): Yo, pull through lp on hook.

Single crochet (sc): Insert hook in st, yo, pull through st, yo, pull through both lps on hook.

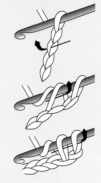

Double crochet (dc): Yo, insert hook in st, yo, pull through st, [yo, pull through 2 lps] twice.

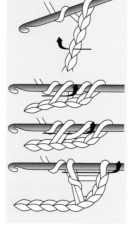

Front loop (front lp) Back loop (back lp)

Front Loop   Back Loop

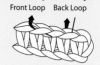

Front post stitch (fp): Back post stitch (bp): When working post st, insert hook from right to left around post of st on previous row.

Back   Front

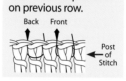

Post of Stitch

Half double crochet (hdc): Yo, insert hook in st, yo, pull through st, yo, pull through all 3 lps on hook.

Double treble crochet (dtr): Yo 3 times, insert hook in st, yo, pull through st, [yo, pull through 2 lps] 4 times.

Slip stitch (sl st): Insert hook in st, pull through both lps on hook.

Chain color change (ch color change) Yo with new color, draw through last lp on hook.

Double crochet color change (dc color change) Drop first color, yo with new color, draw through last 2 lps of st.

Treble crochet (tr): Yo twice, insert hook in st, yo, pull through st, [yo, pull through 2 lps] 3 times.

Single crochet decrease (sc dec): (Insert hook, yo, draw lp through) in each of the sts indicated, yo, draw through all lps on hook.

Example of 2-sc dec

Half double crochet decrease (hdc dec): (Yo, insert hook, yo, draw lp through) in each of the sts indicated, yo, draw through all lps on hook.

Example of 2-hdc dec

Double crochet decrease (dc dec): (Yo, insert hook, yo, draw lp through, yo, draw through 2 lps on hook) in each of the sts indicated, yo, draw through all lps on hook.

Example of 2-dc dec

Treble crochet decrease (tr dec): Holding back last lp of each st, tr in each of the sts indicated, yo, pull through all lps on hook.

Example of 2-tr dec

Metric Conversion Charts

METRIC CONVERSIONS

yards	x	.9144	=	metres (m)
yards	x	91.44	=	centimetres (cm)
inches	x	2.54	=	centimetres (cm)
inches	x	25.40	=	millimetres (mm)
inches	x	.0254	=	metres (m)

centimetres	x	.3937	=	inches
metres	x	1.0936	=	yards

INCHES INTO MILLIMETRES & CENTIMETRES (Rounded off slightly)

inches	mm	cm	inches	cm	inches	cm	inches	cm
1/8	3	0.3	5	12.5	21	53.5	38	96.5
1/4	6	0.6	5 1/2	14	22	56	39	99
3/8	10	1	6	15	23	58.5	40	101.5
1/2	13	1.3	7	18	24	61	41	104
5/8	15	1.5	8	20.5	25	63.5	42	106.5
3/4	20	2	9	23	26	66	43	109
7/8	22	2.2	10	25.5	27	68.5	44	112
1	25	2.5	11	28	28	71	45	114.5
1 1/4	32	3.2	12	30.5	29	73.5	46	117
1 1/2	38	3.8	13	33	30	76	47	119.5
1 3/4	45	4.5	14	35.5	31	79	48	122
2	50	5	15	38	32	81.5	49	124.5
2 1/2	65	6.5	16	40.5	33	84	50	127
3	75	7.5	17	43	34	86.5		
3 1/2	90	9	18	46	35	89		
4	100	10	19	48.5	36	91.5		
4 1/2	115	11.5	20	51	37	94		

KNITTING NEEDLES CONVERSION CHART

Canada/U.S.	0	1	2	3	4	5	6	7	8	9	10	10½	11	13	15
Metric (mm)	2	2¼	2¾	3¼	3½	3¾	4	4½	5	5½	6	6½	8	9	10

CROCHET HOOKS CONVERSION CHART

Canada/U.S.	1/B	2/C	3/D	4/E	5/F	6/G	8/H	9/I	10/J	10½/K	N
Metric (mm)	2.25	2.75	3.25	3.5	3.75	4.25	5	5.5	6	6.5	9.0

Hooked on Crochet! Hats II is published by Annie's, 306 East Parr Road, Berne, IN 46711. Printed in USA. Copyright © 2012, 2017 Annie's. All rights reserved. This publication may not be reproduced in part or in whole without written permission from the publisher.

RETAIL STORES: If you would like to carry this pattern book or any other Annie's publications, visit AnniesWSL.com.

Every effort has been made to ensure that the instructions in this pattern book are complete and accurate. We cannot, however, take responsibility for human error, typographical mistakes or variations in individual work. Please visit AnniesCustomerService.com to check for pattern updates.

ISBN: 978-1-59635-706-8
10 11 12 13 14 15 16

U.S. $8.95 CANADA $10.95

PRINTED IN USA

YRNBK

ISBN: 978-1-59635-706-8